How to Contract with Anyone for Anything

How to Contract with Anyone for Anything

Table Of Contents

Chapter 1:
    Why Outsource?

Chapter 2:
    What Kinds of Jobs Must Be Outsourced?

Chapter 3:
    Finding Professionals to Outsource Your Work to

Chapter 4:
    Getting Professionals from Online Jobsites

Chapter 5:
    Selecting the Right Person

Chapter 6:
    Outsourcing and the Money Equation – Deciding How Much to Pay and How

Chapter 7:
    Outsourcing Milestones and Escrows

Chapter 8:
    The Three Rs that Keep the Outsourcing Tide Flowing – Ratings, Reviews and Relationships

Chapter 9:
    Getting Your Job Done

Chapter 10:
Taking Outsourcing to the Next Level – An Important Step in Online Business Evolution

Introduction

With the amazing popularity that home businesses have achieved in current times, the concept of outsourcing also has become immensely popular. People who want to take their home businesses in a new direction rely on outsourcing to get capable people to team with.

At the same time, even large scale corporations are outsourcing major areas of their work to global professionals.

If there weren't some very considerable benefits involved, outsourcing wouldn't have become as popular as it is today.

This eBook is about how you can outsource your business as well and enhance its productivity several times over.

Chapter 1:

Why Outsource?

Summary

Let us begin by taking a look at why you must outsource your business.

Why Outsource?

Outsourcing wasn't much in vogue until a few years back. In fact, people even thought it quite embarrassing to tell someone that they were outsourcing their work. The general impression was that they weren't up to the task and the unspoken belief was that outsourced work would always be of an inferior quality.

But times have changed. Today, not only has outsourcing become very popular but it has also practically become the norm for businesses. With the grand popularity that home businesses have achieved, the popularity of outsourcing has reached its zenith as well. For, how could a single person working from home carry out all tasks related to a business without depending on a freelancing professional whom they can outsource their work to?

Here are the top reasons why you must consider outsourcing your business:-
- → You can take up more work from a better range of clients because you have an army of people working with you.
- → You can get diversity in your team. When you find different outsourcing professionals, you find that these people are of different qualifications and skill-sets, which means you can even take up work which you were initially avoiding because of your own limitations.
- → You cannot handle all the tasks related with a business alone. There will be several things you are not very conversant with and things that you don't like doing. If that is the case, you might find outsourcing to be a great option to accomplish these tasks adequately.
- → Outsourcing definitely helps you meet deadlines better.
- → For some people, outsourcing is also a means of reducing costs. If a particular service is expensive in your part of the world, you could find a professional from another part of the world where that particular service is cheaper. A lot of people outsource work from the developed countries to

the developing countries where the economic equation helps them reap better savings and stay within tighter budgets.

Most importantly, when you work from home, you might find yourself to be quite lonely, especially when you have to take important decisions. However, when you have intelligent professionals in your team, you do find this task easier.

Chapter 2:

What Kinds of Jobs Must be Outsourced?

Summary

So, what can you outsource?

What Kinds of Jobs Can Be Outsourced?

Any business – whether it is a home business or a large corporate venture – entails a lot of things. With a large business, it is quite easy to see that there are a lot of things involved, but even with home businesses there are various processes, such as the planning aspect, the finding work aspect, the execution of the tasks aspect, the communication aspect, the payment handling and accounting aspect and the further investment aspect. If you are planning to be a home business entrepreneur, you can see that there are various things for you to do. So, which of these can you outsource?

Now, with the Internet making the whole world such a closely-knit domain, you can find professionals to handle all kinds of tasks. They will even plan a whole business venture for you if you have the funds. However, at least initially, you will be on a budget and would like to outsource only things that you really cannot do.

The best idea, then, is to outsource some of the execution aspect of your business. Like, if your home business is about handling content writing jobs, you could outsource the actual writing part. However, the things that are integral for keeping your business going such as planning, obtaining work, communicating with clients, payment handling, etc. should be done by yourself. A lot of people obtain work for higher sums of money and pay a flat rate to writers whom they outsource the work to, keeping the difference as their earnings.

It really helps when you outsource the execution part of your work because of various reasons.
- → The execution part is always the most laborious task. If you are running a website design and development company, the actual designing of the website is the most difficult thing. If this aspect were outsourced, you could focus on getting more clients, while at the same time you are getting the jobs done as well.
- → Also, you can control the execution part better. When some content is written by your employee, you could check its quality and send it back for proofreading or editing if required. When someone designs a logo for your client, you could review it and suggest changes. You can thus supervise these things overall.

When your business grows, you will find that you need to outsource many more things. You might need someone for data entry just to maintain the records of your business. You might need someone just to communicate with your various clients and keep them updated with what's happening. You might need someone to handle the bidding or other routes in which you obtain work. You might even need a virtual manager to handle all these aspects of your business at once.

Know that it is possible to find outsourcing professionals for all your needs, from telemarketing to the complete management of your business. The main thing is in knowing when to use these professionals.

Chapter 3:

Finding Professionals to Outsource Your Work to

Summary

How do you find people to get recruited in your online army of professionals?

Finding Professionals to Outsource Your Work to

Here are a few tips on finding professionals to whom you can outsource your work requirements.

Online Jobsites

The best place to get outsourcing professionals is the online jobsites. The following is a list of 10 of the best of these sites.

GetAFreelancer (http://www.getafreelancer.com/)
ScriptLance (http://www.scriptlance.com/)
EUFreelance (http://www.eufreelance.com/)
eLance (http://www.elance.com/)
Guru (http://www.guru.com/)
RentACoder (http://www.rentacoder.com/)
PeoplePerHour (http://www.peopleperhour.com/)
LimeExchange (http://www.limeexchange.com/)
oDesk (http://www.odesk.com/)
GetACoder (http://www.getacoder.com/)

You will find various categories here. These are job categories. When you have a particular work requirement, all you do is post your project in the relevant job category and people who are interested in accomplishing the task for you will make their bids on it. The concept is quite simple, and because only people who are genuinely looking for work can be found on these sites, you can be sure that you will get your work done.

Forums

There are several forums on the Internet where people put up their work requirements and other people take them up. There is a bidding game involved here as well, but it is not as rampant as on the freelance jobsites. Projects need to be posted as individual threads and interested people make their bids on them. You can also invite particular people to work on your project.

Digital Point Forums (http://forum.digitalpoint.com/) is the best forum where you can find people to handle your jobs for you.

Social Networking Websites

All social networking websites can be looked upon as a potential source to get professionals to handle various tasks. There are groups for freelance professionals on the popular sites. You could become a part of these groups and post your projects.

The following are 3 of the most popular social networking sites where you can find professionals to work for you:-

MySpace (http://www.myspace.com/)
Facebook (http://www.facebook.com/)
Twitter (http://www.twitter.com/)

The only problem with social networking sites is that it is not necessary that these people are looking for work because that is not the primary focus on these sites. Also, there are no systems in place to protect two individuals who work with each other, like you find escrow systems on freelance jobsites.

Chapter 4:

Getting Professionals from Online Jobsites

Summary

Online jobsites are the best places to get your outsourcing professionals. Here are some more details on how they work.

Getting Professionals from Online Jobsites

Since the online jobsites are the best places for you to get professionals, let us look at them in a little more detail.

Here are some of the advantages of getting professionals from here:-
- → People you will find on the jobsites have registered here with the express intention of finding work. Many jobsites are free to join, but some require paid memberships. Being a paid member may reflect a bit more on their sincerity about being professional. Hence, you can be sure you get some sincere people to give your work to.
- → There are various ways in which you can find how good a particular worker is. Every jobsite has a rating and review system (for the employee as well as the employer). This helps you decide.
- → All websites have an escrow system. This takes care of all disputes. Once an escrow is made, the website will arbitrate any problems that arise.
- → You can make detailed project posts, outlining clearly what you want to be done, what time and budget you can afford. People make bids accordingly, so you can be sure you won't have to bargain.
- → You can ask people to show samples of their past work.
- → You can also invite people to bid on your project.

It is very simple to post projects on online jobsites. Many of them, like GetAFreelancer, allow you to post projects for free (though they do take a $5 refundable deposit for each project you post). You only have to post all details of the work as you want it, spell out the timeframe and the budget you can offer and post it in the relevant category.

Once your project is live, which is instantaneous, people start bidding. Then, all you have to do is to look at the bids closely and make your decision on whom to select for your job.

You cannot communicate personally with the bidders till you select them. However, there is a private message board that helps you communicate with them, subject to certain restrictions (like you cannot give out your personal contact details in any way). This helps you decide better about whom to select.

Many people are forging fruitful and long-term work relationships through these online freelance jobsites, irrespective of geographical barriers, and getting mutually benefited. Without the hassle of actually needing employers on their premises, they are able to get their work done professionally and, in most cases, in cheaper ways as well.

Chapter 5:

Selecting the Right Person

Summary

So, how do you go about deciding who the right person to handle your job is?

Selecting the Right Person

When you select your outsourcing professional from a freelance jobsite like GetAFreelancer or ScriptLance or oDesk, there are several ways in which you can make sure you are selecting the right person.

Firstly, you have to ensure that you make all the project details quite clear. Write about everything you expect. These are the things your project post should cover.
- → The nature of your work
- → The amount of work in total
- → Any milestones, like if you want the work to be completed in small chunks and within what frame of time
- → The time you can give for the completion of the whole project
- → The price you are willing to pay
- → Any special qualifications you are looking for in your employees
- → Any characteristics that you don't want in your employees
- → Special points that you will need to make your decision, such as samples.

Most importantly, make sure that you post the project in the right category. People will get alerts only based on the categories they have applied for. So, if you put your project in the wrong category, the right people aren't going to get it.

When you take care to spell out as many details as you can, you can be almost sure that you will get the right people bidding on your work. You may get few bids, but they will be quality bids.

Make sure to check out all the samples of their work, because this is your most important judging point. If you want an original sample, you can mention that in your project post itself and people who are willing to give you an original sample of their work will do so.

In any case, it is a good idea to only post a short-term project initially till you build a trust factor with an employee. Once that is set up, you can go for longer term projects.

Choose people for the following qualifications:-
- → The quality of their work, which you can see through their samples.
- → The ratings and reviews they have obtained on the site.
- → Their responsiveness – It is very important they respond to your emails quickly and it is best if they have an instant messaging id that they can use.
- → Their pricing – Price shouldn't be an important factor unless you are working on a budget.

Once you get a good professional, make sure you pay them promptly and give them a review according to their work. This ensures they will stay with you long and you won't have to undergo the hassle of looking for employees repeatedly.

Chapter 6:

Outsourcing and the Money Equation – Deciding How Much to Pay and How

Summary

Money talk.

Outsourcing and the Money Equation – Deciding How Much to Pay and How

In any business association, money is of paramount importance because that is why business exists in the first place. So, it is extremely important that you have the money equation set right.

The beauty of looking for outsourcing professionals on the Internet is that you can benefit from a very wide range of budgets. Since it is people who are going to bid on your projects, you can select them according to what you can pay. You initially set a ballpark figure of what you can pay and most people will bid within this range.

Whatever your budget is, you are able to find good professionals to work for you within that range. Remember that you are looking at the global marketplace here, and people in other countries may work for much lesser or much higher than what they do for in your local area.

Different jobs have different money equations. It is quite all right if you bid a low budget project initially just to get the feel of the professional's work. You can tell them that you will review payments after you have seen their work. This works well and it also keeps the professional motivated because of the better payments that are poised to come their way.

When you are posting your project on a jobsite, do take some time to check out similar projects that are posted by other people. This will give you a good idea of what you should pay. But, more importantly, you must keep your own budget in focus when posting the project.

Escrows

Escrows help the employer as well as the employed in an outsourcing equation. We shall learn more about escrows in the next chapter.

Online Banks

PayPal (http://www.paypal.com/) is the most popular online bank used by freelance outsourcers. It is followed (though not closely) by Moneybookers (http://www.moneybookers.com/). If you are going to outsource a lot, it is also a good idea to have a Payoneer debit card (http://www.payoneer.com/) since it is affiliated with most of the freelance jobsites including GetAFreelancer, ScriptLance and oDesk. Releasing money from these sites to this debit card does not attract any fees either.

Chapter 7:

Outsourcing Milestones and Escrows

Summary

Milestones and escrows help in building mutual trust factors. Use them well.

Outsourcing Milestones and Escrows

If you want to get the best people working for you, you simply cannot ignore milestones and escrows. Milestones are especially important when you are working on huge projects and want people to give you their deliverables in smaller installments so that you could manage work at your end as well. And we have already seen how escrows are important.

Some websites, like eLance in particular, help you to state the form in which you want your deliverables. You could actually set up milestones for the whole project. Among other benefits, this ensures that your employee can manage the deadline in a much better manner. You can also keep tabs on things better.

It is ideal anyway to post only short-term projects at the start, until you have a rapport set up with the worker. Even though everything might seem all right to you in the bid, there are chances that something might go wrong when the actual project is underway. If you have a long project running, it could be cumbersome to bail out of these difficult situations. However, a short-term project can help.

On GetAFreelancer, the shortest project you can post should be worth $30. However, on most other sites, there is no minimum limit for the project you post.

The best way to make the payment is through an escrow system. Most jobsites work with escrows (which is actually the main reason why you should use these freelance jobsites because an escrow protects both parties). When you select a bidder, you deposit some money into an escrow account. This money is held by the website but not released to the bidder yet. When they accomplish the task, you can direct the website to release the funds to them.

Escrow helps you because in case there is any problem with the project later on and you don't feel like you should pay, you could ask the website to arbitrate. No freelance website will arbitrate if an escrow wasn't made. Also, the worker knows that you have money for the project and it motivates them to do a better job.

Chapter 8:

The Three Rs that Keep the Outsourcing Tide Flowing –
Ratings, Reviews and Relationships

Summary

For long term outsourcing commitments, you need to stretch yourself a little more than the ordinary.

The Three Rs that Keep the Outsourcing Tide Flowing – Ratings, Reviews and Relationships

If you are looking for a long-term outsourcing solution, then the best way to do that is to find one good worker and continue working with them on your future assignments. Even though it seems simple, when you go into the nitty-gritty of employing freelancing outsource professionals, you will find that it is a difficult job. You need a lot of things – commitment, devotion, quality, ingenuity, good price, etc. It is not always that you will hit the jackpot when you are looking at getting work from someone whom you have never met and probably know nothing about their geographical or social position.

That is the reason why once you get a good person to do your job, you must go all out to retain him or her on your outsourcing payroll.

How do you do that? There are three important Rs to remember here.

Ratings

Once a particular assignment is over, you get a chance to rate the professional. This is usually a ten-star rating system on most freelance websites, while even some forums have this system. Don't forget to rate the employee for their good work. For you, it is more important to rate people for their good work than for their bad work. You won't work again with someone who has ruined your project anyway. But when someone does a good job and you commend that with a good rating, they will be happy and inspired to work with you again.

Reviews

Reviews work in the same way as ratings. Only, these are much more elaborate because you say what you feel in words. You could be as upfront here as you like, and don't hold back on mentioning something that you liked. For outsourcing professionals, both ratings and reviews mean a lot – it is akin to having outstanding achievements marked on the résumé of an offline professional.

Relationships

It is also a good idea to have a friendly and frank rapport with a professional who has done a good job for you. Remember that you probably need them more than they need you because there is no dearth of jobs for them. Being a little casual and non-imposing in your communication helps. However, at times, you might need to draw the line, but do so subtly as long as it helps.

Chapter 9:

Getting Your Job Done

Summary

The 'employer' in you should hide till absolutely necessary.

Getting Your Job Done

If you have been following closely until now, there is no reason why you shouldn't get your job done to your satisfaction. But, there are times when difficulties begin to creep in.

One thing that you shouldn't tolerate at all is non-responsiveness. On the Internet, the unsaid rule is that any professional email must be replied to within 24 hours, or sooner if your agreement is to that effect. If you are in the same time zone, there's no reason to wait for 24 hours either. If you don't get your reply within that time, you might as well begin looking somewhere else.

Another thing that is of utmost importance is quality. Even if your outsourcing professional has been providing you good work, do keep checking on it often. Remember that you are not seeing these people. Some of them might pass on their work to cheaper people and work as middlepersons. When that happens, quality definitely goes down.

If you are outsourcing your work, *make it a point to outsource it directly to the person who will execute the job and not to a middleperson.*

Avoid companies unless absolutely necessary. For home businesses, individuals are the best outsourcing professionals. However, if you are a large company and looking for something like a telemarketing agency, then, of course, you need a team of people whom you can outsource your job to.

The two major problems that can happen even after you have selected your professional carefully are non-responsiveness and deterioration of quality. Do not tolerate these problems, or your business will suffer.

Earlier we spoke about keeping a friendly rapport with your professionals. This is fine but only till the time they are providing you consistent good work. If the professional aspect of the relationship begins to wither, you need to tighten things a bit. Let the 'boss' in you show when that happens.

Chapter 10:

Taking Outsourcing to the Next Level –
An Important Step in Online Business Evolution

Summary

About going ahead and making progress.

Taking Outsourcing to the Next Level – An Important Step in Online Business Evolution

When you have built a great rapport with your outsourcing professional who you found one fine day on a freelance work site, you can think on more permanent lines. After all, it is always mutually beneficial to seal professional relationships.

Some companies who don't want to go through the hassle of having to find out outsourcing professionals over and over again go right ahead and build contracts and agreements. These documents are shipped to the address of the professional and they have to sign it and ship it back.

The protection that a contract gives to both parties can help in building better professional collaborations. You won't have to look for outsourcing professionals again; you will have something who you know works in the way you want. Also, the professional won't have to look for clients because they have a contract with you. It is good for the professional to continue working with the same clients over a long term, because they know what the clients require and they also know that they can produce that to the clients' satisfaction.

You might not know it, but a lot of relationships that began casually over the Internet have ended up in the outsourcing professionals shifting their base, even sometimes to other countries, and becoming integral parts of hugely successful companies that they once worked for as mere freelancers. The companies prize these once-upon-a-time freelancers as well because they were with them when the companies were teething, which creates in them a factor of faith and trust.

So, don't hold back on outsourcing your work. You might get one or several faithful and efficient business allies for life.

Conclusion

Outsourcing is the way businesses are moving nowadays, and you must surely make use of this to multiply your business pursuits.

Whatever it is, you can find a suitable outsourcing professional for it.

Now you know what it takes to find one and retain them as well.

All the best to you!!!

www.ingramcontent.com/pod-product-compliance
Lightning Source LLC
LaVergne TN
LVHW020447080526
838202LV00055B/5366